W9-BSF-617

First paperback edition published 1992
by Barron's Educational Series, Inc.

First English language edition published 1982
by Barron's Educational Series, Inc.

All inquiries should be addressed to:
Barron's Educational Series, Inc.
250 Wireless Boulevard
Hauppauge, NY 11788

International Standard Book No. 0-8120-5465-2 (hardcover)
0-8120-1493-6 (paperback)

Library of Congress Catalog Card No. 82-11620

Library of Congress Cataloging-in-Publication Data

Lepscky, Ibi.
   ₍Amadeo. English₎
   Amadeus Mozart / Ibi Lepscky ; illustrated by
Paolo Cardoni; translated by Ruth Parlé Craig.

   22 p.: col. ill.; 27 cm.

   Translation of: Amadeo.
   Summary: Brief text and illustrations recount
Mozart's childhood and the discovery of his
phenomenal musical talent.
   ISBN 0-8120-5465-2 (hardcover)
        0-8120-1493-6 (paperback)

   1. Mozart, Wolfgang Amadeus, 1756–1791—
Juvenile literature.   2. Composers—Austria—
Biography—Juvenile literature.   ₍1. Mozart,
Wolfgang Amadeus, 1756–1791.   2. Composers₎
I. Cardoni, Paolo, ill.   II. Title.

ML3930.M9L43   1982   780'.92'4—dc19   82-11620
                          ₍B₎ ₍92₎   AACR 2 MARC

                                        MN AC

PRINTED IN HONG KONG
5 9927 987654   (Paperback) (Hardcover) 2345 9927 98765

Ibi Lepscky

Amadeus Mozart

Illustrated by Paolo Cardoni
Translated by Ruth Parlé Craig

BARRON'S

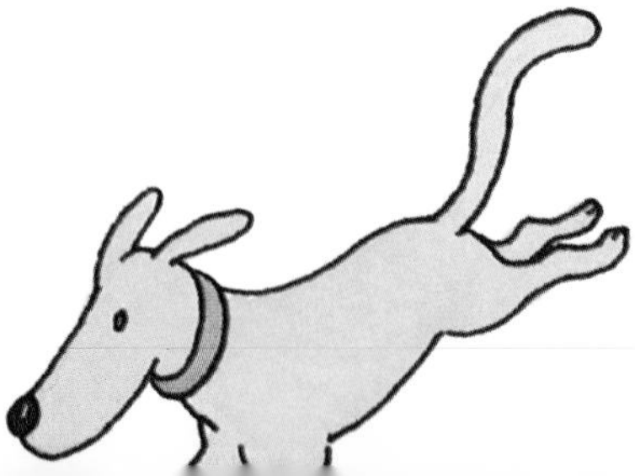

Amadeus was a lively, happy boy. He ran and jumped and chased his sister, Marianna, who was five years older than he. He raced with Pimperle, his little yellow dog, and he played tricks on Teresa, the cook. He loved to be on the move. If someone made him stand still, he would beat his heels together and blink his eyes impatiently.

He liked to play with words. Sometimes he would talk
in a funny way, making up strange little nonsense songs,
like:

> "Ships with big sails
> run before gales
> till the wind fails."

Only music had the power to keep him calm and silent. Whenever his father gave music lessons to Marianna, Amadeus would sit very quietly in a corner without moving, just listening. His mother would sigh with relief.

Then one day Amadeus suddenly climbed up on the piano bench and played a minuet his father had just taught Marianna. He played the song perfectly, without hitting one wrong note and without ever having had a lesson.

And so his father, who was an expert in music, realized that Amadeus had a great talent for music and an amazing musical memory.

From that day on, Amadeus' father gave him violin and piano lessons every day. Amadeus learned easily and soon surpassed Marianna in skill.

Marianna, who adored her little brother, was not
jealous of his success. Instead, she was very proud of him.

So was Amadeus' mother, who especially enjoyed the
perfect little sonatas that he composed.

After a while, Amadeus' father, proud of his son's
accomplishments, decided to let everybody know of his
wonderful child. And with that decision, the life of young
Amadeus became almost a fairy tale.

At age seven, when other children were attending school, Amadeus was traveling with his father and sister to all the royal palaces of Europe. Across the land, he was admired and applauded by emperors and empresses, kings and queens, princes and princesses.

At that time, in the courts of Europe, royal families seemed to be competing to give the most beautiful parties, the most unusual shows. They held one event after the other—dances, masquerades, theatricals, concerts. And they were always looking for something special to present. So when they learned about young Amadeus and his spectacular talents—his ability to repeat on the violin and piano very difficult music he had heard only once and to compose on the spot magnificent musical pieces, everybody wanted to see him, hear him, and applaud him.

For his royal concerts, Amadeus wore an elegant suit, blue satin shoes with golden buckles, and a little sword on his side. He looked like a miniature cavalryman. Marianna accompanied him proudly on the piano.

Often, when he played the violin, ladies in the audience would bend forward and stare at him through their opera glasses, to make sure that Amadeus was really a child and not a dwarf. At a concert in Italy, before playing for the king and queen, Amadeus had to take a ring from his finger because the people thought it might be the magical cause of his extraordinary abilities.

11

But Amadeus' accomplishments were definitely not the result of magic. And despite his powdered wig and cavalryman costume, he was definitely a child. He traveled among emperors and empresses, kings and queens, and he received applause, admiration, and fine gifts.

Did all this attention make Amadeus conceited? Did the splendor of the courts blind him to everyday fun? No, Amadeus remained the same boy as before. After the concerts and the applause, he played with the little princes and chased the princesses, just as he chased Marianna and Pimperle at home.

At night, Amadeus would not go to bed until he had sung to his father a funny little song full of words he had made up. He called it

"Oragnia Fitafagnia."

At the end, he would kiss his father on the nose.

Also, Amadeus created his own imaginary kingdom. He named it the Kingdom of Rücken, and he was its king. In Rücken, every citizen was good and faithful. Amadeus even designed a map of his imaginary kingdom and named all of its cities, rivers, and mountains.

No, success did not spoil Amadeus, and the splendor of the courts did not blind him. The music that was in him was a great gift, a gift that he appreciated and that far outshone everything else in the world.

But while Amadeus, his family, and certain other wise people recognized the richness of Amadeus' talents, many did not. They saw only the sensational side of his performances, not the artistic side. So sometimes his concerts were announced like this:

Because of overwhelming enthusiasm,
Amadeus Mozart will today,
August 30,
perform one additional,
final concert for your amazement.
Just six years old,
the child will not only play on the piano
and the violin the most difficult music of advanced teachers,
but will also play a violin concert and piano symphonies
with the keyboard covered with a felt cloth.
In addition, he will correctly name
from a distance all notes played,
separately or in chords,
on the piano or on bells,
glasses, or other objects.
And finally he will improvise on the piano
and the organ in all the most difficult keys.

To the people reading such announcements, young Amadeus was considered an amusing show. He was enjoyed, like the jugglers, acrobats, and tightrope walkers who sometimes performed with him.

"Little Mozart is an impressive child, that's all!" said a very learned critic.

Fortunately, Amadeus' father realized that all the traveling and all the exhibitions were preventing the boy from developing his marvelous creative qualities.

Also, Amadeus was growing tired and no longer had his pink cheeks and lively ways.

So his father decided to bring Amadeus home.

"Good," said Amadeus. "I will go back to my Kingdom of Rücken." And without regret, he left the sparkling courts of Paris and London and Vienna, left the applause and admiration, and returned home with his father and sister.

His family was happy to see him. Pimperle barked in joy. Teresa prepared him a cake. And his mother embraced him tenderly.

At home, Amadeus did not just play. He wanted to write down all the music he had in his mind so it would not be lost. He spent hours at his desk.

His father, who felt responsible to God for the artistic education of such a gifted son, designed a course of study for Amadeus. It was difficult and demanding.

But young Amadeus worked hard. He explored many fields of music. He created new styles of expression. He achieved new heights of beauty and perfection.

And in time, Amadeus wrote some of the world's most beautiful music and became one of the greatest composers who ever lived—Wolfgang Amadeus Mozart.